WordPress For Beginners

"How to Quickly Set Up Your Own Self Hosted

WordPress Site and Domain for Beginners - All

For Under $25 – Plus Real World Tips & Tricks

To Save You Time & Energy"

Positive Impact Books
7579 E. Main Street
Suite 500
Scottsdale, AZ 85251
www.PositiveImpactBooks.com

Legal Disclaimer:

Table of Contents

Chapter 1 - WordPress 101: The Wonders of WordPress

WordPress is a web software that you can use to create your website or blog. It was written in PHP programming language. Since it was released in 2003, it became one of the most popular web publishing platforms. Today, it supports more than seventy million websites and growing.

But, what a lot of people don't know about Wordpress is that it is more than just a blogging tool. It is also a flexible and powerful content management system or CMS. It allows you to build and manage your own website using your web browser! It is powerful, easy to use, and most of all – it's an open source project. This means that it's free because hundreds (if not thousands) of volunteers all over the world are constantly improving its code.

WordPress allows people to build a website without writing a single code. It is open source, this means that the code behind the software is available and openly shared with whoever who wants to improve it. It is supported, maintained, and developed by a community and not by a company.

Benefits of WordPress

Even if WordPress was created a decade ago, developers are still raving about it. And to be honest, nothing comes close to it. Here's a list of the top benefits of using WordPress as your content management system (CMS) software:

WordPress has polished features.

WordPress is definitely one of the best content management and website builder platforms. It has polished features that allow you to create a personal blog or website in just a few minutes.

1. It is easy to use.

You do not have to be a seasoned programmer to use WordPress. If you know how to use a computer and run any Microsoft office program, you can create a website using WordPress.

WordPress allows you to launch a professional website quickly without coding. In fact, you can launch a website in just a matter of hours. If you want to get into the web design business, WordPress is a great place to start.

2. It has an extensive functionality.

It has a wide plugin directory which we will discuss later on. This allows you to easily, quickly, and inexpensively add functionality to your website. If there's any feature that you want to add to your website, there's a way to do that without coding or spending money. You can add a calendar or sell digital products, you can simply add that feature to your WordPress website.

3 It is FREE.

If you're a small business owner, you would want to save money and take advantage of anything that's free. WordPress is a powerful website builder and content management system that's free. You do not have to pay for anything out of pocket. You just have to pay for the domain name and hosting.

4 It is flexible.

You do not have to wait for your web developer. WordPress allows you to make changes to your website yourself. Since you don't have to wait for a few days for your web designer to make the changes, you can quickly alter the content of your website.

5 It is SEO-friendly.

Your website is no good unless it is visible in the search engine results page of Google or Yahoo. SEO or search engine optimization is a process of making your website visible on the search engine results page by targeting specific keywords. Now, this concept is too complex or intimidating for small business owners.

WordPress takes a lot of the complexity of SEO and makes sure that all your website pages are set up in a way that your potential clients will easily find you on Yahoo, Google, or MSN.

6 WordPress allows you to add multiple users.

As the administrator of a WordPress site, you can add multiple users to help manage your site.

7 It allows you to create mobile-friendly website.

You do not have to create a second website for mobile users. WordPress automatically recognizes if a website visitor is using a mobile device or a web browser.

8 It allows you to manage your time.

WordPress allows you to add multiple posts and schedule them to publish on your website over a twelve week period. This allows you to manage your time well.

9 It allows you to connect your website content to your social media account.

WordPress automatically integrates your blog posts to your Twitter, Facebook, and even, LinkedIn account.

10 You'll have a fast learning curve.

Here's what's awesome about WordPress – it's easier to use than Microsoft Word. You can learn how to post new pages, edit content, and add photos in just a few hours. You can learn how to use WordPress by watching YouTube tutorials.

11 It is secure.

Many people think that WordPress is not secure, because it is an open-source software. But, the opposite is true. This content management system is secure because of the diligent efforts of the members of the WordPress community.

Hundreds, if not thousands, of programmers are working to improve its security each day. This is the reason why WordPress has endured a number of high profile attacks over the past few years.

12 It allows continued readership.

WordPress is so easy to use that it encourages you to post content regularly. This encourages web users to repeatedly visit your site. WordPress automatically integrates RSS feeds – a software that increases your readership.

RSS stands for Really Simple Syndication. It is a way for blog readers to track the content of different websites in one news aggregator. The biggest benefit of RSS is continued readership. It allows readers to continue reading your content without visiting your website.

To access your RSS feeds, you just need to go to www.yourdomainname.com/feed.

13 It is popular.

WordPress runs on more than 60% of self-hosted websites. It is massive, huge, and reliable.

Core Features

It is not an exaggerating to say that WordPress is like the Holy Grail of web development. Programmers and web developers around the world love WordPress because of its amazing features which include:

Application Framework

WordPress can help you build apps, too. It has a number of features that you can use to build apps like HTTP requests, user management, translations, databases, and URL routing.

Custom Content Types

WordPress has a number of default content types. But, it is also flexible as it allows you to create metadata, taxonomies, and custom post types.

Theme System

WordPress is known for its theme system. The WordPress application program interface (API) helps to create both simple and complex themes.

WordPress themes are innately multipurpose so you can use for multiple websites. You can use a single theme for different platforms, so it allows you to save money. The theme system comes with a demo and they are packed with "ready to use" shortcodes. This means that you can create a theme even if you do not know how to code. You can even use this system to create eCommerce codes.

The Latest Library

WordPress has a library filled with useful scripts such as Backbone.js, jQuery, Plupload, and Underscore.js.

Plug in System

What's amazing about WordPress is that it has a plug in system. This means that you can add certain functionalities to your WordPress website.

Wordpress plugins are also written in PHP programming language and they can be integrated seamlessly into your website.

Wordpress has a powerful but easy to use system that allows you to install and uninstall plugins from the admin area of your website. You can also download and manually install the plugins using FTP client.

There are thousands of Wordpress plugins. In fact, you can add plugins for many uses like social media, galleries, images, security, and SEO. We will discuss the more popular ones in the later part of this book.

Wordpress websites are easy to build and manage. Anyone who can use Microsoft Word can build a WP website. It is portable which means that you can use it from any type of computer and it is SEO friendly, too. This means that WP websites have the ability to perform better in various search engines like Google or Yahoo.

It also helps to save time and money. Let's face it, dealing with a web developer is challenging and often frustrating. If you use WordPress, you can build and manage your site yourself, so you do not have to hire a web developer. You also do not have to waste time communicating to your web developer to request for site changes.

Most of all, WordPress has an awesome blog feature that's easy to use and maintain. WordPress is a powerful tool that you can use to create and manage website.

Chapter 2: What is PHP? (Static HTML Websites vs PHP-Based Websites)

As mentioned earlier, WordPress is a PHP website. It is an acronym for Hypertext PreProcessor. It is the most commonly used open source scripting language and it can be embedded into HTML. It allows you to create scripts and web pages.

PHP is a server-side scripting language that was developed in 1995. This means that the code is executed on the server side and not on the client side. It allows you to create web pages that are NOT static.

Before we discuss PHP and differentiate it from HTML, let's discuss what HTML is. Well, HTML is the acronym of HyperText Markup Language. It is the backbone and the structure of a website. It is one of the core components of the internet along with other front-end machineries such as JavaScript and CSS. It is technically a set of symbols and characters that tells the internet how to display a page's text or image. Each markup code is called an element, but it's popularly known as a "tag".

Here's a list of common HTML tags:

<body> - Defines the body of the text

<h1> to <h6> - Heading tags

 - Single line break

<html> - HTML document

<strong> - Defines important content

<form> - HTML form

<audio> - Defines audio content

HTML is the markup language. Most web designers use HTML with a combination of other markup and scripting languages to create web pages for a website. Typically, a web developer uses JavaScript, HTML, and CSS to build a website.

HTML websites are static. This means that the information does not change and it remains the same for every site visitor. The content of HTML websites is stored in static files. It has a static content, organization, and structure.

HTML websites require low or no maintenance. You do not need to regularly back up or install updates. You can just create a backup once and then, just forget about it. You do not need servers with installed PHP or MySQL. This means that the website can run on cheaper servers.

But HTML websites are very difficult to update. In fact, you'd need a formal training in programming to update an HTML website. You would need to hire a developer to make even the slightest changes like updating old content, adding new pages, or uploading images.

HTML websites have no additional features. If your business grows and you want to add an online store or a gallery, you would need to hire a developer to do this and that developer may recommend that you migrate your website to WordPress or some other variation of a PHP-driven website.

HTML websites operate on cheaper servers. But, since you need to hire a developer to do even the smallest tasks, the cost of maintaining an HTML website is usually higher than maintaining a PHP website.

PHP is a back-end scripting language. Today, the majority of websites runs on PHP because of the popularity of PHP content management systems (CMS) such as Joomla, Drupal, and WordPress. Websites that are built using the PHP are linked from an HTML file. A PHP code is enclosed in special start and end processing instructions such as <?php and ?>.

A PHP code looks like this:

```
<!DOCTYPE HTML>

<html>

    <head>

        <title>Example</title?>

    </head>

    <body>

        <?php

            <echo "enter command";

        ?>

    </body>

</html>
```

PHP is executed on the server as opposed to client-side scripting language such as JavaScript. It is a back-end scripting language while HTML is a front-end markup language. This means that PHP uses HTML code as a structure.

PHP is very easy to use and learn especially if you are acquainted with the syntax or Perl or C. You can write a command using a few line codes. This gives you maximum control over your website. PHP is open source so it is free. You do not need to buy an expensive software to use it. It allows you to build a website at a minimal cost. It also has more functions than HTML.

It is cost efficient and reliable, too. It is also platform independent which means that it supports all major browsers and operating systems. It has faster processing speed than other scripting languages. So, it allows you to develop web apps like CRM or eCommerce. Using PHP is one of the most secure ways of developing websites and apps.

PHP is easy to read. This means that you do not have to be a coding genius to understand what the code is. It is clean and organized. It is also flexible so it's easier to add a new code without having to worry if it is in the correct place. It is easy to edit and it has better performace than most programming languages.

When you use PHP on your site, you don't have to think about programming so much. So, you can focus on the design of your site. And to top it all, it's free and easily available.

The main advantage of using a PHP-based website is that it has **dynamic content**. It is easy to update. You can simply log in to your WordPress site and add a new page without hiring a web developer. It has an intuitive user interface that makes it easy to update and create pages.

PHP-based websites such as WordPress have professional ready-to-use templates that are developed by professionals all over the world. These sites are powerful. You can create contact forms, add a reservation system, and add a photo gallery by installing plugins. You can make whatever changes that you want.

HTML	PHP
Acronym of Hypertext Markup Language	Acronym of Hypertext Preprocessor
It is a markup language that cannot perform computations.	It is a general purpose programming language.
Front-end technology	Back-end technology
Used to create static sites	Used to create dynamic websites
HMTL-based websites are hard to modify.	PHP-based websites are easy to modify.
It is client-based.	It is server-based.
You need to hire a web developer to maintain your site and make changes.	You can make website changes yourself.
Too complicated.	Easier to learn and execute.

If you do not have all the technical training, it's best to use PHP-based websites. These websites are easy to use and navigate. You also do not need a skilled web designer to build your PHP site. You can simply use an open-source PHP software like WordPress to build and design your dream website.

Chapter 3 - WordPress.com Versus WordPress On Your Own Hosted Domain Account

WordPress is an open-source publishing platform that makes it easier to publish content online. It powers millions of websites. There are two types of WordPress – WordPress.org and WordPress.com. The major difference between the two WordPress platforms is who's hosting your website.

When WordPress was initially launched, it was an open-source content management system. But, years after it was launched, Matt Mullenweg (the co-founder of WordPress) noticed that a lot of users are clamoring for a built-in WordPress hosting service. So, to meet this demand, he created WordPress.com – a managed and shared hosting services.

WordPress.com is a fully hosted website. It allows you to build your site free of charge if you choose the basic plan which goes with the ".wordpress.com" extension. You can also avail of the WordPress business hosting plan which comes with premium hosting, custom domain, and backups. This platform gives you access to hundreds of themes. It even allows you to install your custom theme.

If you are using a WordPress-hosted website, you can integrate your site with social networking sites such as Tumblr, Twitter, and Facebook. This site also comes with popular features such as comments, stats, polls, and sharing. If you use the basic site, there's no need to install plugins. To use a WordPress-hosted website, you have to register an account with WordPress.com.

When you use a WordPress-hosted website, you technically do not own the website. This means that WordPress can turn off your website if it goes against their terms of service.

WordPress.org is also known as the "real WordPress". It is a website platform that you can use on your own self-hosted website. It is open-source and it is free for anyone to use – you just need a web hosting account and domain name. This is the reason why WordPress.org is also known as a self-hosted WordPress. This allows you to get your hands dirty. You just need to purchase a domain name from a third party vendor like

GoDaddy.com, sign up for a hosting account and install Wordpress within the account control panel.

The WordPress CMS is free and it is really easy to use. You own your website and its data. You do not have to worry about your site being turned off. You can customize your web design as needed. You can add paid, free, and custom WordPress plugin to your website.

The biggest advantage of running a self-hosted WordPress site is that you can actually use your site to earn money. You can run your own ads without sharing your revenues with someone else.

You can also use a self-hosted WordPress to build an online store. You can use it to sell physical or digital products. You can accept PayPal and credit card payments. You can also ship the goods directly from your website. You can also use this website to create membership sites. You can sell memberships for courses and content. You can also use it to build an online community.

WordPress.Com	WordPress.Org
WordPress.com is a hosting service.	WordPress is a content management system.
WordPress is free. But, you should adhere to the terms and conditions. WordPress can turn off your website anytime if they feel that your website is not following their guidelines.	WordPress.org is a software that you can download and install on your web server.
It comes with a free domain name called ".wordpress.com". You can also get a custom domain for a specific charge.	You would have to purchase the domain name from a third party provider.
WordPress.com comes with built-in features, but you cannot install plug-ins.	You can install plugins.
It comes with polished themes.	It comes with polished themes.
It comes with personal support. When you create a WordPress account, you also have access to WordPress forums. If you sign up for the premium plan, you'll get live chat and email support.	You need to visit the WordPress.org forums to ask for assistance.
You must register to build your WordPress.com account.	No registration needed.

So, which one should you choose? Should you go for WordPress-hosted website (WordPress.com) or a self-hosted WordPress website? Well, it depends. If you're into blogging, it's a good idea to get a WordPress-hosted website. But, if you plan to use your website for business, Defintely choose the self-hosted route.

Chapter 4 - Domain Registration

In this section of the book, you'll learn all about domain registration. You'll know what a domain name is. You'll also learn the different domain name types and how to choose the right one for your website. This chapter also contains a step by step guide on how to purchase a domain name from one of the most popular domain registrars – GoDaddy.com.

Domain Name Explained

Each website has an address called domain name. Your website's domain name serves as the site identification. It identifies your internet resource – computer, service, or network. It is easier to memorize than the numbered addresses used in the internet protocols (IPs).

Domain names were created to make IP addresses more human friendly. The IP address is the unique set of numbers that are assigned to every computer on the internet. It is basically like a street address. They identify where a computer is located. A regular IP address looks like this – 191.179.3.95. It's not easy to memorize, right? While computers can easily identify IP addresses, we humans can use domain names.

The Domain Name System or DNS creates domain names that people easily understand like www.facebook.com or www.twitter.com. The DNS then translates that name to numbers so computers can understand them. So, instead of memorizing 66.220.144.0, you can simply type www.facebook.com. Easy, right?

When people types your domain name in a web browser, the browser (such as chrome or internet explorer) uses your domain name to find your website IP address. Then, it passes back the website associated with that IP address.

Your domain name serves like the contacts that you store in your cellphone. So, when you tap the contact on your mobile phone, your phone automatically dials the number associated with that phone. You do not need to know where the person you're calling is located to enter their specific phone number. All you need to do is just tap the contact name and the phone does the rest.

The primary domain is simply the domain that you use to buy your server – like businessname.com. It is the name that you would register for your business or your website. A domain name is usually referred to as a primary domain or the top level domain. A primary or top level domain is a name that you choose to represent your business. It will be yours for a specific time (one year, five years, or ten years). Nobody else can touch it for that specific time.

You have the freedom to point this domain name to whatever site you want. You can use this name to represent you or your business. So, you have to pick a domain name that's short, stand-out, and easy to remember. It's also a good idea to pick a domain name with .COM as that's what people would generally associate with a business.

Once you have a primary domain, it's also a good idea to get a number of other domains as well to get more online traffic to your site. Adding secondary domain names also protects you from people who try to register your business name with other extensions to try to steal away your business. You can acquire a number of other domains. You can use .ORG to post internal company updates. You can use the .BIZ to showcase the business side of your company.

The first step in setting up and installing your self-hosted WordPress website is to make a decision about your domain name (which is also known as the unique resource locator or URL). Then, you have to purchase that domain name through a domain registrar. When you "buy" a domain, you really don't own it. You just earned the right to use it for a specific amount of time (one year or up to ten years).

Most domain registrars give you the choice to avail of a service called "autorenew". This automatically renews your domain once it expires and then charges the fee to your credit card.

Domain Syntax and Extensions

A URL typically has three parts:

http://www.facebook.com

The protocol is how your browser should communicate with a server when opening your website. The most common protocol is HTTP or hypertext transfer protocol. Another common protocol is HTTPS, which means hypertext transfer protocol secure. The HTTPS protocol is usually used by e-commerce websites. There are also a number of less common protocols such as imap (internet message access protocol), pop (post office protocol), and ftp (file transfer protocol).

Domain Types

As discussed earlier, the domain name is the unique human friendly identification of your IP address. It has a domain extension that represents the purpose of your website or the location of your business.

Here's a list of the domain types:

1. **Generic Top Level Domains** – These domains are at the highest level of the domain name system structure. .COM is the most popular domain name extension. You should choose this extension if you want your website to look legit. More than fifty percent of websites use a .com extension.

2. **Generic Restricted Top Level Domains** – These domains are a bit similar to the generic top level domains, but the use is a bit restricted. For example, .BIZ is restricted to business and .PRO is reserved for accredited professional.

3. **Sponsored Top Level Domains** – These domains are sponsored and proposed by organizations and private agencies. It has strict rules on who could use these extensions. For example, .AERO is reserved for the members in the air transport industry.

4. **Country Code Top Level Domain or ccTLD** – Country code top level domain extensions are usually made of two characters such as .UK or .AU.

5. **Reserved Top Level Domains** – Top level domains such as .INVALID or .TEST are reserved by IANA or Internet Assigned Numbers Authority.

6. **Second Level Domain** - This website type is below the top level domains. It usually contains two extensions. For example, universities may use the .AC.UK website extension, such as the University of Oxford website www.ox.ac.uk. Companies may use the .CO.UK extension, such as www.amazon.co.uk.

7. Third Level Domain – These domains are directly below the second level domain.

Examples of Country Code Domains

Zimbabwe	yourdomain.zw
Egypt	yourdomain.eg
South Africa	yourdomain.za
Belize	yourdomain.bz
Slovakia	yourdomain.sk
Switzerland	yourdomain.ch
Cook Islands	Yourdomain.ck
Zambia	yourdomain.zm
Samoa	yourdomain.ws
Vanuatu	yourdomain.vu
Andorra	yourdomain.ad
China	yourdomain.ca
Guam	yourdomain.gu
Armenia	yourdomain.am
Greece	yourdomain.gr
US Virgin Islands	yourdomain.vi
Uruguay	yourdomain.uy
Italy	yourdomain.it
British Virgin Islands	yourdomain.vg
Venezuela	yourdomain.ve
Germany	yourdomain.de
Hong Kong	yourdomain.hk
Spain	Yourdomain.es

Norway	yourdomain.no
Puerto Rico	yourdomain.pr
Cayman Islands	yourdomain.ky
Iceland	yourdomain.is
Iraq	yourdomain.iq
Philippines	yourdomain.ph
Kiribati	yourdomain.ki

Examples of Location-Based Second Level Domains

As mentioned earlier, second level domains have two extensions. The first extension usually indicates the website's function. The second extension contains the location of the website, e.g. www.greepeace.org.au. But, in some cases, the first extension represents the state where the organization is operating. The second extension indicates the country where the organization is located e.g. qld.au (for websites located in Queensland, Australia).

.asn.au	For associations, clubs, and political parties in Australia
.com.au	For business in Australia
.org.au	For the non profit organizations in Australia
.edu.au	For educational institutions in Australia
.act.au	For businesses and organizations located in Australian Capital Territory
qld.au	For businesses located in Queensland, Australia
.commerce.fr	For websites in France
.parliament.nz	For offices, parliamentary agencies, and political parties in New Zealand
.law.za	For lawyers and law firms in South Africa
.gov.ua	For government agencies in Ukraine

Tips on Choosing A Domain Name

Here's a list of tips that you can use in choosing a domain name:

1. *Make sure that it's easy to type.*

Choosing the right domain name is critical to the success of your business. So, make sure that your domain name is easy to remember and easy to type. Keep your domain name short and straight to the point.

2. *Insert keywords into your domain name.*

Keywords are the words or phrases that people use to find things on the internet. If you want your potential clients to easily find you, insert keywords in your domain name. For example, if your company name is Alva and you're selling shoes, it's a good idea to include "shoes" in your domain name. So, instead of "www.alva.com", you may want to go for "www.alvashoes.com". This way, it's easier for your potential customers to find you.

3. *Target your local area.*

If you run a local business, it's a good idea to include your city or state in your domain name. For example, if you run a plumbing company in Utah, you can choose www.utahplumbing.com as a domain name.

4. *Do not use hyphens and numbers.*

Hyphens and numbers are hard to type. So, as much as possible, avoid using them.

5. Use the right domain name extension.

Domain name extensions are suffixes found at the end of a website address such as .net or .com. These extensions have specific functions, so choose the one that works well for your company or organization.

The .com extension is the most popular one. But, it's kind of hard to get a memorable .com domain name because the best .com site names are already taken. So, you may want to consider the following alternative domain name extensions:

- ✓ .biz – You can use this if you're building an e-commerce site.
- ✓ .org – If you run a non-profit organization, you should consider this website extension.
- ✓ .net – This is for technical sites.
- ✓ .info – This extension is for informational sites.
- ✓ .co – This website extension is best for companies, communities, and even e-commerce sites.

6. Use a domain name generator.

If you really have a hard time coming up with a domain name, you can try domain name generators such as DomainHole, Lean Domain Search, or Wordoid.

If you are starting a personal website or a blog, it's a good idea to use your name. This will help you build your personal brand and make you more popular, if you are ok with putting your personal name out there like that.

How To Buy A Domain Name

There are a number of domain registrars that sell domain names such as GoDaddy, Sedo, Flippa, NameCheap, iPage, FatCow, Hover, Gandi, Dreamhost, and Name.com.

But, because GoDaddy is the most popular domain registrar today, let's discuss the step by step process of purchasing a domain using GoDaddy.com.

1. Log in to GoDaddy.com.

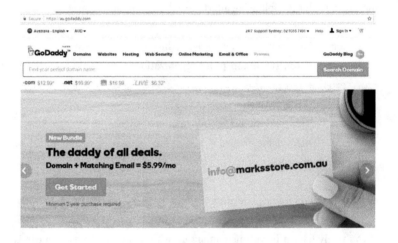

2. Now, type your desired domain name in the "find your perfect domain" space.

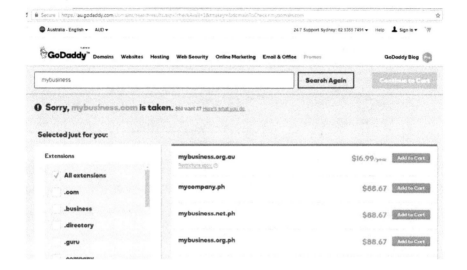

3. If your desired domain is already taken, you'll find suggested domain names on the left side of your screen.

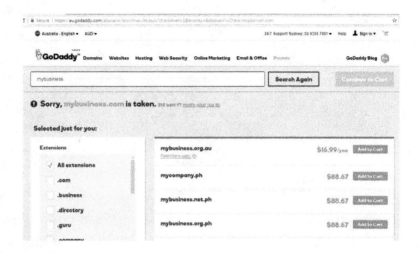

4. You'll see the price beside each domain name. Choose the one that fits best for your business and your budget.

5. Once you've chosen the right domain name, click on "add to cart". Then, click on the orange "continue to cart" button.

6. You'll see the web page below. If you want extra security, click on the Privacy Protection radio button. But, if you don't want any of that, just click on the radio button beside "No Thanks".

Scroll down to
continue to cart
↓

We've added privacy. Here's why.

When you register a domain, regulations require your name, address, email and
phone number to be published in a public directory. Privacy hides your information,
protecting against spam, scams and more. See example ⑦

We highly recommend domain privacy, but it is an **optional** feature.

Select plan

⦿ **Privacy Protection** $7.99 /domain per year
View details ⑦ $14.99

◯ **Privacy & Business Protection** $21.99 /domain per year
View details ⑦ $57.96

◯ **No Thanks**

7. If you want to create an email that matches your domain, then scroll down and choose the email plan that's best for you. If not, choose "No Thanks".

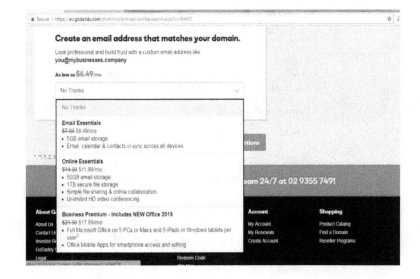

8. When you're done, click on "continue with these options".

9. You'll see the summary of your order. Check the terms. How many years do you intend to own your domain name? Is it one year? Or two years? If you're not too attached to the domain name, you can choose to rent it for one year. But, if you feel like you'd need it in the long run, then it's best to rent it for two years or more.

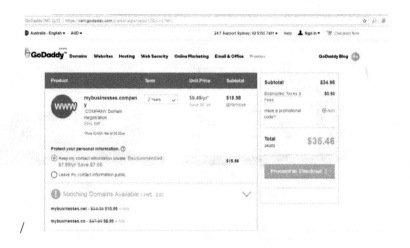

10. Once everything is okay, click on "proceed to checkout".

11. You'll need to sign in to proceed with the order. If you do not have an existing GoDaddy account, you have to click on "create an account".

12. Now, after you created an account, you'll need to pay for your order. You can pay using a credit card, a debit card, or PayPal.

13. Now, once you've entered your payment info, you're good to go. You now own your domain name for a specific amount of time.

Now, that you've successfully acquired a domain name, it's time to choose a web hosting provider.

Chapter 5: Select A Web Hosting Provider and Set-Up Your Hosting Account

To make your website visible on the internet, your data and files must be stored in a computer that's connected to the internet. These computers are called web servers. Website hosts are companies and organizations that house several web servers in one location. This is often called a data center.

Hosts provide the security, tools, support, and bandwidth that connect your website to the internet. It is like a mall that contains several stores. If you want to open a shop at a mall, you need to lease a space. Just like a mall, hosting companies allow you to lease a space in their web servers where you can store your website files and make them available for visitors.

Web hosts offer a number of hosting solutions. You can choose the one that fits your server space need and the amount of "bandwidth" that you would need each month. Bandwidth is simply the amount of data being transferred at a given amount of time.

If your website does not need a lot of space, then you can rent a small server space. But, beyond server space and bandwidth, there are other things that you should consider in selecting a hosting solution. You need to consider your budget and the ease of use. You also need to consider the level of flexibility and customization. You may also want to consider the privacy and security features in choosing the right hosting solution for your website.

Types of Web Hosting Solutions

There are four main types of hosting solutions:

1. Shared Hosting – If you choose a shared hosting solution, your account is one of the many accounts on a server that's maintained by a hosting company. A shared server is like an apartment building with several tenants. This hosting solution is cheaper. But, an influx of traffic to one website on the server will affect the bandwidth of the other websites. So, this is a good choice for low-traffic websites.

   If you have a limited budget, shared hosting may be the best option. This solution is perfect for a website that does not have more than two thousand visitors daily.

2. Virtual Private Servers or VPS – A VPS, as the name suggests, is a virtual server that's private. Unlike shared hosting, a VPS hosting has a guaranteed allotment of system and resources that only you have access to, but everyone is still on the same physical machine/host.

3. Dedicated Hosting – Dedicated server hosting is best for websites that generates a lot of traffic daily like Facebook or Twitter. It is known as the "Rolls Royce" of web hosting. If shared hosting is like renting an apartment and VPS is like renting a townhouse, dedicated hosting is like renting an entire house.

   It is a step above VPS hosting. It is also the most expensive type of hosting. So, unless your website is drawing at least one hundred thousand visitors per day, it's not practical to choose dedicated hosting.

4. Cloud Hosting – Cloud hosting is a hosting service where the files are stored in the cloud. If you choose cloud hosting, your files are backed up in multiple locations. What's amazing about cloud hosting is that you only pay for what you use. But, it is prone to service outages. So, you would expect some downtime

every now and then. Also, you have limited control over your services, data, and applications.

Shared hosting is cheap. It is perfect for small businesses. If you want to establish a website for less that $25, it's best to go for shared hosting. But, if you're looking to attract a lot of visitors in the future, it's a good idea to choose VPS hosting. It is less expensive than the dedicated server, but it gives you all the bandwidth that you need.

Best Hosting Providers

Web hosting is now becoming a common commodity. It's no wonder that the number of hosting companies increases by the minute. But, here's a list of the most reliable web hosting providers:

1. HostGator

HostGator offers shared hosting plans for as low as $2.99 per month. Plus, they have an uptime of around 99.98%. They also have a friendly and proactive technicians that provide support. They have a user friendly control panel and a free site builder. They also offer a 45 day money back guarantee.

2. BlueHost

Most BlueHost plans come with a free site builder and domain. They adhere to the highest hosting hardware. They also have an awesome customer support team.

3. Site Ground

This web hosting provider offers plans that include CDN, email, SSL, and daily backups. Their lowest plan has about 10 GB web space and it is suitable for websites with ten thousands visits per month.

4. InMotion Hosting (#1 Author's Pick)

InMotion Hosting is convenient because it comes with pre-installed WordPress. Their plans usually include unlimited bandwidth and a free SSL certificate. They have solid reputation and they have a team of friendly and competent customer service staff.

5. HostPapa

This company provides affordable, but reliable web hosting that uses green energy. They offer user-friendly tools that anyone can use. They also have an impressive 99.9% uptime. Then, they have a thirty day money back guarantee.

6. Dream Host

Dream Host has been around for almost two decades. Up until today, they are still one of the most reliable web hosting providers. They power over five hundred thousand WordPress blogs. They do not collect a set-up fee and they offer a free domain, too.

7. GreenGeeks

They have a hosting platform that's easy to install and manage. They provide a 24-hour support and they come with free domain name.

8. A2

A2 provides fast and reliable WordPress hosting. They also have a team of technical experts that can help with your needs.

9. Pagely

This is the largest WordPress hosting platform and it is now powered by Amazon cloud. They are used by big companies such as Twitter, Facebook, and Microsoft.

10. GoDaddy

Yes, GoDaddy offers hosting, too, that costs only $1 a month! Their yearly plan also comes with a free domain. It's awesome, isn't it?

11. Site5

This web hosting provider offers special plans for those who are new to WordPress. They offer superb support and service. Their servers are located in various cities around the world including London, Sydney, Singapore, and Amsterdam.

12. Ipage

This company was established in 1998 and they have been providing reliable and fast hosting services since then. They offer unlimited hosting that comes with a free domain.

Purchase Your Hosting and Set Up Your Hosting Account

There's a long list of reliable web hosting provider which includes Hostgator, A2 Hosting, SiteGround, Bluehost, Ehost, A Small Orange, Site5, and InMotion. For the purposes of discussion, let's discuss how you can purchase and set up an InMotion hosting account.

1. Go to the website of your web host provider. In this case, go to www.inmotionhosting.com.

2. Click on "get started" now.

3. This will take you to the shared hosting options. Choose the option that works well for you and then click on "order now".

4. VPS is a better option, especially if you're planning to establish a high traffic website. Go to www.inmotionhosting.com/vps-hosting if you wish to purchase VPS hosting. But, please take note that this is expensive. So, unless you're planning to create a website that attracts as much traffic as Buzzfeed, it would be a good idea to go for shared hosting. You can always upgrade your hosting plan later on.

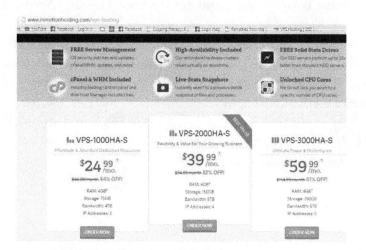

5. Select your preferred hosting term. You could either purchase 1 month, 6 months, or 1 year hosting.

6. Choose the data center you like (East Coast or West Coast).

7. Click on "I already own this domain" and enter your domain.

8. Enter your email address and click on "continue".

9. Fill up your billing information.

10. Click on "review my order".

11. If everything is good, then you're done.

12. Log in to your account management panel.

13. Go to www.inmotionhosting.com. Click on "log in" at the top right corner of your screen.

14. Since this is your first time to log in, click on "click here".

15. This will take you to the "forgot password" page. Enter your domain name and your email address, then click on submit. You'll receive a password reset link through email.

16. Check your email and click on the link. This will take you to this page.

17. Enter your new password and click submit.

18. Click on the log in link. Then, type your email address and your password.

19. Now, you're logged in to your account management panel! This allows you to create a cPanel account and then easily manage your website.

The Account Management Panel or AMP is the gateway that gives you access to any tool that you need. This allows you to update your billing information, access your cPanel, install software, and renew your subscriptions. Remember that your AMP contains your credit card number and other billing information. Do not give this information to your web developer or someone you don't trust.

Chapter 6 - cPanel Basics: What Is It and Why It's Good to Gain Further Knowledge Of Its Functions

cPanel is a linux-based online hosting control panel. It has a graphical interface and tools that are intended to streamline the web hosting process. It uses a three layer structure that allows the web developers and owners to control the different parts of their blog or website. cPanel is designed to function as a virtual private server or a dedicated server.

It is the industry-standard and it is used by most web hosting companies. It makes web hosting account management easier. It is easy to install and also easy to use. You don't need to be a coding genius to learn how to use cPanel.

It is a low-maintenance program and it only requires 20GB disk space. It has a top notch email management function. It also comes with anti-virus and anti-fraud protection.

So, what does cPanel do? Well, it helps create and manage e-mail address. It also allows you to create and manage files. It also helps you create and manage databases.

Benefits of cPanel

cPanel is amazing. It is free and it's used by Linux-based web hosting. Here's a list of the cPanel benefits that you can use to your advantages:

1. It is easy to install and use.

You do not need to be a computer genius to install and use this web hosting management system. It has an intuitive graphical interface that allows you to do tasks like looking for web directories, calculating disk space, making regular back-ups, and site maintenance in just a few clicks.

2. It saves money.

Because it is easy to use, you do not have to hire people to maintain your site. You can do it yourself. So, you'll definitely save a lot of money on labor costs.

3. It's compatible with all browsers.

You can run this program using any browser – Chrome, Safari, Mozilla Firefox, or Internet Explorer.

4. It's compatible with software add-ons.

What's amazing about this hosting management system is that it's compatible with third party software add-ons. It supports apps and add-ons such as calendars, guest books, bulletin boards, and blogs.

5. It's reliable.

cPanel is so reliable that it automatically restart the system once it detects a failed service. It also has a domain name system (DNS) clustering system. This improves the performance of your hosting system and minimizes downtime.

6. It's portable.

This is one of the most amazing features of the cPanel. It is moveable. This means that you can move your website from one hosting company to another without any problem.

How To Create A cPanel Account

Now we know how awesome cPanel is. But, how do you login to your "cPanel"? Well, it's kind of easy. You just have to follow these steps:

1. First, log in to your hosting account management panel. If you're using InMotion hosting, log in to secure.inmotionhosting.com/index/login.

2. Then, click on the cPanel icon.

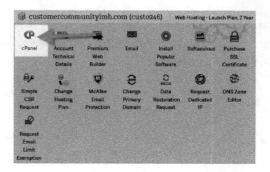

3. This will take you straight to your cPanel. You do not need to enter a username or password.

4. If it does ask you for a username and password. Just click on "back" and then click on the "account technical details" button.

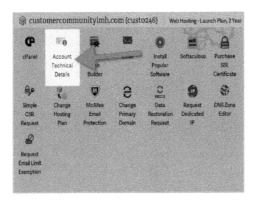

5. You'll see your username and password. Take note of that and then, click on the cPanel icon. Use your username and password to log in.

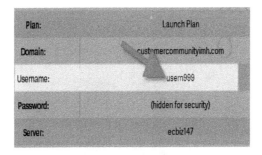

If you're working with a team of web developers and bloggers, it's best to log in to cpanel by typing **yourdomainname.com/cpanel**. Then, you'll see this page.

If you have not pointed your domain name to your web host server yet, type this in your web browser yourservername.yourdomainname.com/cpanel, example ezbiz143.example.com/cpanel. Then, enter your username and password.

Chapter 7 - Quick CPanel Tutorial (How to Point Your Domain to the Web Hosting Account)

Now that you have purchased a domain and you already have a web host, it's time to point your domain to your web hosting account. You need to follow two basic steps – change the nameservers and then add the domain name to your web host server. The good news is it just takes a few minutes to do this.

In the earlier sections of this book, we discussed how to purchase a GoDaddy domain name and use InMotion hosting. So, now, let's discuss how to point your GoDaddy domain to your InMotion hosting.

1. First, you need to log in to your InMotion hosting account. You'll see a screen that looks like this:

2. Go to your "cPanel".

3. You'll see this:

4. Look for the shared IP address which is located at the bottom left part of your screen.

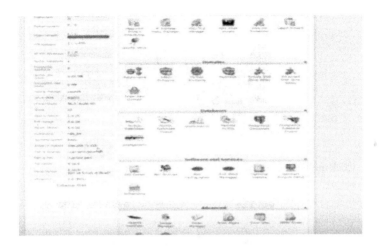

5. Highlight and copy the IP address at the lower left side of your screen.

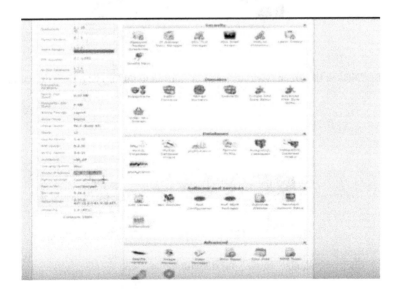

6. Then, log in to your GoDaddy account.

7. Click on the drop down menu beside your name.

8. Click on the green "visit my account" button to pull up your domain names.

9. Click on "manage" to see your domain names.

10. Type the domain name you want to direct on the search tab at the upper right side of your screen. Then, click on "search".

11. Click on the drop down next to the domain name.

12. Click "manage DNS".

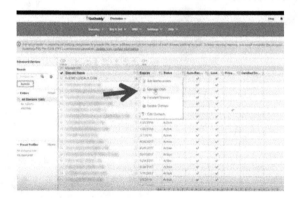

13. You'll see the DNS records of the chosen domain name.

14. Look at the "host record" section and then click on "edit".

15. Under "host to", paste the IP address from your InMotion hosting account.

16. Click on "finish".

17. Then, click on "save changes".

18. Your domain name is now on your InMotion hosting account.

19. Go back to your cPanel.

20. Click on "addon domains" button.

Source: greenmonkeymarketing.com

21. Click on the domain name you want to add.

Now that you have successfully added your domain name to your hosting account, it's time to install WordPress.

Chapter 8 - cPANEL: Making A Database In MySQL

cPanel allows you to create and manage a database. You can use this database to run a website and store files.

To create a database in MySQL, you need to follow these steps:

1. Go to your "cPanel".

2. Under databases, click on MySQL database.

3. You'll see this page.

4. Enter the name of your database and then, click on "create database".

5. You'll see this page. Enter your desired username and password. Then, click on create user.

6. If you want to add more users in your database, you can click on "add users". You can always remove these users anytime you want.

You're done. It's that simple!

Chapter 9 - CPANEL: How to Add-On More Domains You Register To Your Account

You can operate multiple websites/domains in your cPanel account. This feature is especially useful for businesses that operate multiple websites. If you own a business with multiple brands, you need to add more domains to your hosting account by following these steps:

1. Go to your "cPanel". Enter your username and password.

2. Go to the "domains" section.

3. Click on the "addon domains" button.

4. Under create an addon domain, enter the domain name that you're going to add to your cPanel account.

5. There's a default subdomain so you won't need to type a subdomain name.

6. You'll need to enter the "document root". This is the folder where you store the files of your domain, ex. public_html/domain.com.

7. Click on the button that says "create FTP account". This is helpful if you are working with a web developer who needs FTP access.

8. Click the "add domain" button.

9. You'll see this page.

10. If you click on back, you'll see your domain listed on addon domains.

You're done! You're ready to set-up your other website.

Chapter 10 - How To Install WordPress Using Softaculous

Earlier in this book, we've discussed how useful it is to install WordPress in your self-hosted website. In this chapter, you'll finally learn how to install WordPress on your website using a wonderful tool called softaculous.

Softaculous is an amazing tool that runs on your cPanel or other control programs such as Plesk and DirectAdmin. It allows you to install a number of customer support software, eCommerce software, and blogging platforms. It also allows you to install WordPress on your self-hosted website. You can do this by following these steps:

1. Go to your "cPanel".

2. After you log in, scroll down and go to the software services section.

3. Click on the "softaculous" button.

4. You can see the top applications in Softaculous and click on the WordPress icon.

5. Then, click on the "install" button.

6. Under "choose protocol", you have the option to choose between the following options:

- http://
- http://www.
- https://
- https://www.

You can go with whatever you like. The https option provides added security to your website. But, you would need to purchase an SSL certificate to use this protocol. We will discuss this later in the bonus section of this book.

7. Below the "choose protocol", you'll see "choose domain". If you have multiple domains in your hosting account, you'll need to choose the website where you want to install WordPress.

8. Leave the "in directory" section blank.

9. Enter your database name under the "database name" section. The name usually starts with wp_, ex. wp_01.

10. Under site settings, enter your website name.

11. Enable multisite if you plan to operate multiple blogs in your website. We will discuss this feature later on in the bonus section of this book. If you decide to use the "multisite" feature, make sure to use plugins that are compatible with multisite.

12. Enter your desired admin username and password. This is what you'll use when you log in to your WordPress CMS and dashboard. Make sure to use a unique admin name and a strong password. We will discuss the password rules under the bonus section of this book.

13. Enter your admin email. You'll get an email every time someone comments on your blog or there's updates available.

14. Choose the language you want to use.

15. Under select plugins, click on the "limit login attempts". This feature can protect your website from hackers by limiting the login attempts. You can also install this plug in later, after you complete the installation process.

16. **Click on the "advanced option". You'll see a number of options there. Should you want WordPress to automatically upgrade your themes, click on "auto upgrade WordPress themes". If you want WP to automatically upgrade your plugins once a new WP version comes out click on "auto upgrade WordPress plugins". You can add these options later after installation.** We'll discuss this process later in the bonus section of this book.

17. After you've chosen all of your preferred options, click on the "install" button located at the bottom part of your screen.

18. Below the install button, enter your email address so you'll get a notification once the installation is complete.

19. The installation takes a few minutes. Once it's complete, you'll see this page.

20. You'll see a link that points to your website. When you click it, you'll see this clean and blank installation of WordPress.

21. You'll also find your admin URL. This is where you log in to your posts and manage your blog, photos, and other content. When you click on that URL, you'll see this:

Log in using your admin name and password. Now, you can start creating your website content!

Chapter 11 - How To Install WordPress Manually Using A Free FTP Utility

It's quite easy to install WordPress by using your cPanel. You can also install it using a free FTP utility like **Filezilla**. But, to do this, your web host must be able to support MySQL and PHP. You'll also need the ability to create MySQL databases. You'll also need an FTP software like Filezilla. You'll also need to have your web hosting username and password.

You can do this by following these easy steps:

1. Go to filezilla.project.org. Then, click on "download now".

2. Then, install it on your computer.

3. Now, you'll need to get a hold of the WordPress files. To do that, go to wordpress.org. Then, click on "Download WordPress".

4.

5. Download WordPress to your computer.

6. Go to your web hosting panel by typing yourdomainname.com/cpanel in your web browser. Scroll down and make sure that you can see the "MySQL Databases".

7. Unzip your WordPress files.

8. Now, you're going to see this.

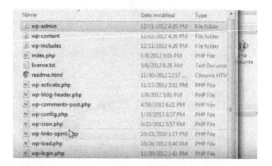

Name	Date modified	Type
wp-admin	12/11/2012 4:20 PM	File folder
wp-content	12/11/2012 4:20 PM	File folder
wp-includes	12/11/2012 4:20 PM	File folder
index.php	1/8/2012 5:01 PM	PHP File
license.txt	5/6/2012 8:28 AM	Text Docume
readme.html	11/30/2012 12:57	Chrome HTM
wp-activate.php	11/17/2012 3:11 PM	PHP File
wp-blog-header.php	1/8/2012 5:01 PM	PHP File
wp-comments-post.php	4/10/2012 6:21 PM	PHP File
wp-config.php	1/20/2013 8:57 PM	PHP File
wp-cron.php	9/23/2012 5:57 PM	PHP File
wp-links-opml.php	10/23/2010 1:17 PM	PHP File
wp-load.php	10/26/2012 8:40 PM	PHP File
wp-login.php	11/30/2012 1:41 PM	PHP File

9. Select all the files. Then, go to FTP filezilla.

10. Enter your host which is ftp.yourdomainname.com. Then, enter your username and password which is the same as your cPanel access.

11. Click on the "quick connect" button.

12. Click on public_html. This folder holds your website files.

13. Select all the files that you downloaded from WordPress.

14. Drag and drop these files to your FTP.

15. While FTP is uploading your files, go to MySQL.

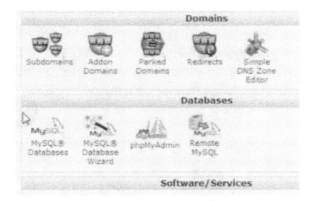

16. You can click on MySQL databases. But, it's better to click on the MySQL Database Wizard because it's easier to use.

17. Now, create a database. Enter your preferred data base name on the space next to "New Database".

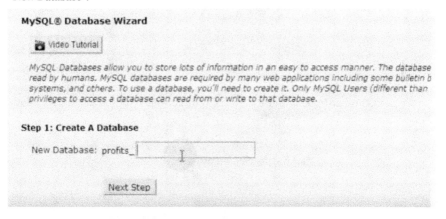

18. Click on the "next step" button.

19. Enter your preferred username and then, click on the password generator to get your password. Make sure that you save your password in a safe location.

Added the database profits_db.

Step 2: Create Database Users:

Username: profits_

Note: seven characters max

Password:

Password (Again):

Strength (why?): Very Weak (0/100)   Password Generator

20. Click on create user.

21. You'll see this page, click on "all privileges".

22. Now, go back to your FTP. You'll see that your WordPress files have been uploaded.

23. It's time to start the installation process.

24. Now, type http://www.yourdomainname.com/wp_admin/install.php on your web browser. This will start the installation process.

25. Now, you'll see this page. Click on "create a configuration file". Then, click on "let's go".

26. You'll see this page.

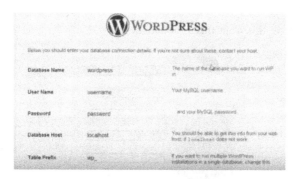

27. Now, enter your database name and your password.

28. Your database host should be local host and the table prefix should be "wp_".

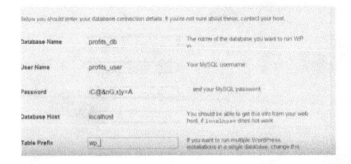

29. Click on "submit".

30. You'll see this. Copy this information.

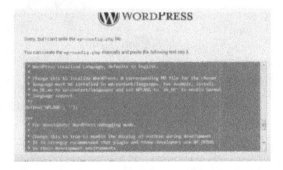

31. Then, go to your computer files and right click on wp_config.php. Click on open with Word Pad. Select all and delete.

32. Now, copy everything on WP file to your wp_config.php file.

33. Click on "save".

34. Now drag your wp_config.php file from your computer to your FTP.

35. Then, click on "run install".

36. Now, enter your site title, admin name, preferred password, and email address.

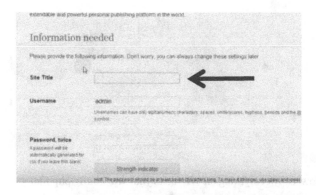

37. Once you're done, click on "Install WordPress" located at the bottom of the screen.

38. This will start the installation process. Once done, click on "log in".

39. Enter your username and password.

Now, you can start posting!

Chapter 12: Installing Themes – Free Themes and Theme Clubs

There are hundreds of free WordPress themes. These themes are perfect for bloggers, small business, and even e-commerce sites. These themes are incredibly responsive. This means that it looks good in any device – desktop computer, laptop, tablet, and smartphones.

But, how do you install themes? Well, it's quite easy.

1. Log in to your WordPress account.

Photo Source: shoutmeloud.com

2. Go to "appearance".

3. Go to "themes".

4. Click on "add new".

5. Click on "upload theme".

6. Choose the free theme that you like. Then click on "install now".

7. You'll see this page. Click on the "preview" link to see how your site will look like with the new theme.

Ⓦ Instant WordPress

🔲 Installing Theme from uploaded file: thesis_182.zip

Unpacking the package...

Installing the theme...

Theme installed successfully.

Preview | Activate | Return to Themes page

Photo Source: shoutmeloud.com

8. Click on "activate".

Free WordPress Themes

You do not have to break the bank to use WordPress themes. There are hundreds of themes that you can use for your WordPress site. But, here's the list of the best ones:

1. Sydney – This theme is clean and professional looking. It's best for businesses. It is translation ready. It includes social links and it allows you to add a slider header which is really cool.

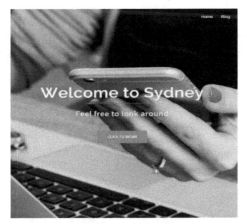

Photo Source: codeinwp.com

2. ShopIsle – This has a widgetized footer and a responsive contact form. It is also translation ready and it is WooCommerce ready. It is perfect for those who want to build an online store.

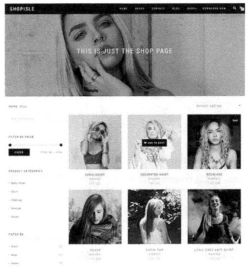

Photo Source: shopisle.com

3. Allegiant – This is an elegant theme that's perfect for all kinds of business. You can use it to showcase your portfolios. You can use it for both startups and big companies.

Photo Source: shopisle.com

4. Flash - Flash has a full width slider that has a clean and responsive design. It has color options and it comes with a flash toolkit plugin. It also has great product filters.

5. Palmas – This theme has a dainty design that's perfect for writers who want to showcase their work. It has a featured slider and it is optimized to increase site speed.

Photo Source: shopisle.com

6. ReviewZine – This theme has a responsive design. It has an attractive slider, too, and it supports several languages. It has a widgetized footer and it has an elegant, modern design.

7. Parallax One – This theme has a simple design and it has a parallax effect. It comes with attractive logos, menus, and icons.

8. OnePress – This theme has a clean and responsive design. It has a parallax effect and it supports WooCommerce.

9. Astrid – This is perfect for small business owners. If you want to showcase your portfolio, this is the perfect WP theme for you.

10. Spacious- This theme has a minimalist design. It has a responsive slider and it is compatible with WooCommerce.

11. Restaurant Theme – As the name suggests, this is perfect for restaurants.

12. Bento – This theme is perfect for graphic artists who want to showcase their designs. It has a flexible layout and it's compatible with WooCommerce.

13. Amadeus – This theme has a modern design and it is SEO-friendly. It has an elegant feel and a minimalist design.

14. Everly Lite – This theme is perfect if you plan to have SEO work done on your site. It has a responsive layout and it is widget ready.

15. Lavander Lite – This has a responsive design and it has multiple posts. It also has a minimalist design that's clean and elegant.

16. Point – This has a responsive design and it comes with custom widgets.

17. Azera Shop – This theme is perfect for online stores and even blogs. It is compatible with WooCommerce.

18. Kale – This theme has cool sliders that you can use to showcase your products.

19. Virtue – Virtue has a beautiful art gallery that's perfect for portfolios and online shops.

20. Simple – As the name suggests, this theme has a simple design. It is SEO-friendly and photo-friendly.

21. Magazine – This theme is perfect for magazine-like blogs who feature celebrity stories. It is clean and it comes with more than forty layout choices.

22. Corporate Plus – As the name suggests, this theme is perfect for corporate websites.

There are hundreds of other awesome and free themes that you can use. Just go to https://wordpress.org/themes/.

Theme Clubs

Theme clubs provide premium WP themes on membership basis. If you choose to become a member of one of these theme clubs, you'll have access to high quality WordPress themes. The membership is usually renewed every month or every year. These club offers professional quality designs and live front-end demos. They also provide customer support to members. These clubs usually offers designs for specific niches like businesses or online store.

Here's a list of the best theme clubs:

1. WooThemes
2. **Elegant Themes (Authors Best pick – Click Here To Join!)**
3. NattyWP
4. Templatic
5. StudioPress
6. Obox
7. WPZOON
8. Obox
9. Upthemes
10. Themify

Theme clubs are useful for web designers who develop multiple websites. If you plan to create just one website, it's not practical to join a theme club.

Chapter 13: Adding and Editing Menu Items

One of the best things about WordPress is that you can customize almost everything about it. To increase your productivity and efficiency, WP allows you to add, remove, and edit your menu items.

To do this:

1. Log in to your WordPress using your username and password. This will take you to your dashboard.

2. Hover over "appearance" which is located at the left side of your screen.

3. Now, when you see the sub-menu, click on "menus".

4. Select the menu that you would like to edit. You may have different menus depending on how your website was designed. But, most WordPress websites have two menus – the footer menu and the main menu.

5. You'll see the menu structure. On the upper left side of your screen, you'll see the list of all the pages and services that you can add to your menu.

6. Now, click on the box next to the item that you want to add to your menu.
7. Click on the "add menu" button.

8. Now, the item is already added to the menu.

9. To edit the structure of your menu, you can just click and drag items into the place that you want to put it in.

10. You can also make an item a submenu by clicking, dragging it, and placing it below under its "parent menu item". Sub-menus are usually indented to the left.

11. To edit the menu item label, just click on the drop-down menu on the right side of the item. This allows you to edit your navigation level. You can also click on "remove" if you wish to remove this item from the menu.

12. Once you're done editing your menu labeling and structure, click on "save menu".

Now, you have a customized and gorgeous menu!

Chapter 14: Plug In Basics

One of the biggest advantages of using a self-hosted wordpress is the ability to install and use plugins. Plug ins are additional functionalities that you can add to your WordPress website.

Plugins allow you to customize and expand the functionalities of your website. These plugins allow you to add beautiful galleries, forms, calendars, SEO tools, social media sharing buttons, and more awesome stuff to your website.

There are thousands of free plugins in the Word Press Plug In Directory like Contact Form 7, Akismet, Yoast SEO, WooCommerce, Limit Login Attempts, and Duplicate Post. There are also a number of paid plug ins.

But, why would you want paid plugins? Well, paid plugins are usually maintained by a team of developers and support staff. These support staff can help you with compatibility issues **and also keep the security patches up to date which is very important with a Wordpress site**.

How To Install WordPress Plugin

There are three ways to install a plugin:

- ✓ Automatically install the plugin through WordPress.
- ✓ Manually upload the plugin via FTP.
- ✓ Manually upload the plugin through a medium like a server set-up.

The easiest way to install a plugin is to do it through WordPress. You can do this by following these steps:

1. Log in to your WordPress by entering your user name and password.
2. Now, go to plugins and click on the "add new" link.

3. This will take you to the "install" screen. Now go to the "search" section and type the plugin you want to install. Click on "search plugin".

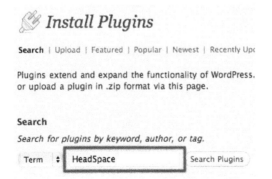

4. You'll see this. Click on "install".

5. Once you're done, click on "activate plugin".

You're done! It's that simple!

Best WordPress Plugins

After WordPress was launched, hundreds (if not thousands) of web developers have created plugins that increases the functionality of a WordPress site. So, there's literally thousands of WordPress plugins, but here's the list of the best plugins that you should install in your self-hosted website.

1. WordPress SEO by Yoast

A good website content is nothing without enough search engine visibility. To increase the visibility of your website in the search results pages of Google or Yahoo, it's a good idea to install the WordPress SEO plugin to your website.

This plug in allows you to easily add title tags and meta tags on your posts. It is incredibly easy to use. When you are writing the meta information for your post, this plugin gives you a preview of the Google result snippet. This way, you'll see exactly how your post looks like when someone search for it on Google.

This plugin helps you create site maps that support images. It also notifies the search engines once your post is published.

It has other awesome features like:

- ✓ Focus keyword testing
- ✓ Permalink cleanups
- ✓ XML news sitemaps
- ✓ Robots.txt editor
- ✓ .htaccess editor
- ✓ Improved canonical support
- ✓ Redirects setups
- ✓ Video tutorial

2. Backup Buddy

This is a powerful plugin that helps you setup a reliable backup timetable for your site. You can use this plugin to save your content backup in multiple locations such as your computer, a cloud storage service, or an FTP server. It allows you to sleep soundly at night knowing that all your website posts are safe and backed up.

3. WPForms

Building website forms usually take time. WPForms has an easy "drag and drop" system that allows you to create contact forms, order forms, email subscriptions, and payment forms in just a few minutes.

This plugin allows you to create 100 percent responsive forms. This means that your forms look good on all types of devices – laptop, desktop computer, tablet, and mobile phones. This plugin has a number of pre-built workflows and form templates so it's definitely easy to use.

4. Disqus

This powerful commenting system is best for high traffic websites. This is a third party commenting system that does not affect your server so it does not affect your site loading speed. It also has anti-spam filters so it automatically filters out spam comments and blocks out the autobots.

5. Login Lockdown or Loginizer

To protect your site from hackers, install login lockdown to your self-hosted site. Most hackers rely on a long list of passwords to break into your website's admin area. This plugin limits the login attempts on your website. It locks down the admin area of the website for a limited time after a number of attempts.

6. OptinMonster

This plugin helps you cash in your website by converting casual website visitors into email subscribers (marketing leads). This plugin helps you to grow your email list.

7. Sucuri

Security is one of the biggest problems of online business owners. Sucuri is a plugin that protects your website from malware threats, DDOs, brute force attacks, XSS attacks, and other types of attack. It is basically a firewall that you can easily integrate into your self-hosted site through WordPress.

8. Soliloquy

Sliders are attractive and you can use to showcase your company's products. It allows you to display your products, featured content, and announcements in an interactive way. The sliders are translation ready so it's great for international audiences. It has a simple drag and drop system that makes it user friendly.

9. CSS Hero

WordPress themes are created via cascading style sheets (CSS). CSS allows you to customize the look of your website.

CSS Hero is a plugin that allows you to customize a WordPress theme without writing a code.

10. Beaver Builder

This plugin allows you to build a landing page without learning how to code. It is a drag and drop page builder tool that you can use. Aside from the Beaver Builder, you can also use a number of other drag and drop website builder plugins such as Elementor, Divi, and Themify Builder.

11. Hummingbird

People do not stay on websites for more than 8 seconds. If it takes too long for your site to load, visitors would most likely leave your site before they get to see what your site is about.

Caching can speed up your site. This is where Hummingbird comes in. This plugin scans your website and checks site issues. It allows you to check the overall speed of your site and fix some issues.

12. Edit Flow

Do you run a syndicated blog? Then, this plug in is perfect for you. EditFlow allows you to easily collaborate with your editorial team. This plugin has a lot of awesome features such as:

- Custom Status
- Calendar
- Notifications
- Editorial comments
- User groups
- Story budget

13. Floating Social Bar

If you want to increase your social media shares, this is the perfect plugin for you. This is a social media plugin that allows you to add a number of social networks.

14. AdSanity

This plugin allows you to manage your ads – the short codes and the widgets.

15. WPtouch

This plugin allows you to create a mobile version of your website. This plugin has a built-in support for mobile advertising, eCommerce, and custom content.

16. Jetpack

This plugin was created by the people who are behind the WordPress software. Jetpack strengthens the security of your website.

17. Akismet

This plugin provides a status history of each post comment so you'd know which comments are spam.

18. Redirection

This plugin helps you manage your 301 redirections and keep track of your 404 errors. Redirection automatically adds a 301 redirection whenever you change the permalink of your posts. But, you can also use this plugin to manually add 302, 307, and 301 redirections.

19. Mailchimp

Mailchimp is one of the popular email marketing services in the market today. It allows you to send emails, track results, and manage subscribers. This tool is perfect for small business owners who are trying to get more leads.

20. Envira Gallery

You can easily create beautiful galleries in WordPress. But, Envira Gallery allows you to create responsive and beautiful galleries through their user-friendly interface.

Plugins are fun, useful, easy to install, and most of them are free! These plugins allow you to save money, increase your site efficiency, improve your productivity, increase your website visibility, and maybe help you earn more revenue.

Chapter 15: How to Add and Edit Pages and Posts

WordPress has a user-friendly system that allows you to easily add and edit your website pages and posts. You do not need to have a degree in computer science or web design to learn how to edit and add pages and posts.

How to Add and Edit Pages

To add and edit pages, you need to follow these steps:

1. Log in to your WordPress dashboard and then click on "content".
2. You'll see a drop-down menu, go to website pages.
3. Now, click on the "create a new website page" button.
4. Once you're done, you'll need to choose a template for your page. Go to the template menu located at the left side of your screen.
5. Choose the template that you like. Enter the page name and then, click on "create".
6. Now, below the page title, type your content.
7. Once you're done. Click on "settings" at the top center portion of your page.

Photo Source: knowledge.hubspot.com

8. You would see this page. Type in your page name, page title, page URL, and meta description. The page name is the internal name for your page while the page title

is the one that will appear on the page. The URL is the link that appears on the users' browser when they visit the page.

The meta description is the content that appears below the link in the search engine results page of Google or Yahoo. It is the description of what the page is about. We'll discuss this in detail in the later part of this book.

If you wish to run an ad campaign, click on the "select campaign" menu.

Basic Info

Page name ⓘ

About Us

Page title ⓘ

About Us | doyouplag.com

Page URL ⓘ

http://www.doyouplag.com ▼   about-us-doyouplag.com

Meta description ⓘ

Learn more about the team of writers and content creators for doyouplag.com

Great, you're within the limit 80 remaining

Campaign

Select a campaign   ▼   Add new

Photo Source: knowledge.hubspot.com

9. Once you're done click on save.
10. To increase your website traffic and improve your online presence, it is necessary to do SEO on your site. SEO is search engine optimization and it is the process of increasing your ranking on search results page (SRP) of the top search engines like Yahoo and Google.

To optimize your page, go to the SEO section and then, click on the "bar   graph" icon.

Under the "this website page is about", type in your targeted keywords. For example, if you sell women's shoes in New York, it's best to target the keywords "shoes New York", "women's shoes in New York", and "New York women's shoes". The keywords are the words or phrase that potential customers type on Google to find businesses like yours.

11. Click on the "eye" icon located at the left side of your screen. Click on "device preview" to see how your website looks like on desktop computers, laptops, smart phones, and tablets.

12. If you're satisfied with how your page looks like, click on "publish" or "schedule".

If you wish to publish the post right away click on "publish now". If you wish to schedule the post some other time, click on the blue "schedule" button.

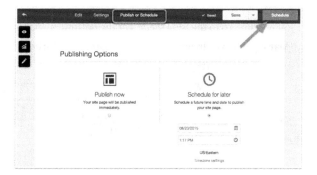

Your new website page is now ready!

How To Add and Edit Posts

Now, it's time to add a post by following these steps:

1. Go to your dashboard.

2. Now, click on "posts" located on the upper left side of your screen. A sub-menu will appear, choose all posts.

3. You'll see the list of all your posts.

4. To add a new post click on add new.

5. Enter your blog title and content.

6. Once you're done, go to the SEO section at the bottom of your page. This section will appear if you have already installed the **Yoast SEO plug in.**

Photo Source: ShoutMeLoud.com

7. Go to the left side of your screen. Add a new category. If you're writing about "yoga" for example, you can add "yoga" category.

8. Below the categories, you'll see tags. Tags make your posts searchable so make sure to add your "keyword" as your post tag. For example, if you're a chiropractor in San Francisco writing about the benefits of going to a chiropractor, you may want to add relevant tags such as "chiropractor" or "alternative medicine".

Photo Source: siteground.com

9. Click on edit next to your permalink – the link to your site. You want to keep this short and relevant to your post.

Photo Source: ithemes.com

10. Click on "preview" to see how your site looks like.

Photo Source: WPsamurai.ph

11. If you're satisfied with how your site looks like, click on the blue "publish" button.

Now, if you wish to edit your post, follow these steps:

1. Click on "posts" located at the right side of your screen.
2. A sub-menu will appear, click on "all posts".
3. You'll see all your posts.

Photo Source: HostMonsteraccount.com

4. Click on "edit" below the title of the post you want to edit.

5. Edit your post.

6. Once you're done, click on the "preview changes" button.

Photo Source: kidscodecs.com

7. If you're satisfied with the changes, click on the blue "update" button at the right part of your screen.

Your post is now updated!

Chapter 16: Use the Screen Options Menu At the Top

The screen options is a menu that's located at the top right corner of your WordPress dashboard. This will help you add extra stuff in the admin area of your WordPress account.

Your screen option should look like this:

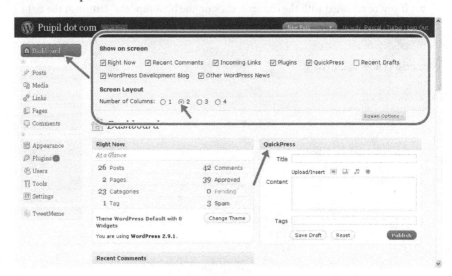

There's a lot of search options. You just have to click the ones that are useful for you. Then, click on apply.

Chapter 17: How To Create A Page Dedicated to Blog Posts

WordPress supports a popular blogging system that top bloggers use. But, if you use your website for different purposes like e-commerce, portfolio showcase, and blogging, you may want to create a separate page for your blog posts.

You can do so by following these steps:

1. Go to your dashboard.

2. Click on "pages" at the left side of your screen.

3. A sub-menu will appear, click on "add new".

4. Under title, type in "Blog".

5. Now, go to the template located at the right side of your screen. Choose a template that you like or you can always go with "default template" which comes with your theme.

6. The comments are automatically enabled, but if you want to disable it just uncheck the "enable comments" box.

7. Click on publish.

8. Now, you need to separate your blog page from the rest of your website pages.

9. Click on settings. You'll see the "reading settings" page.

10. Under the front page, choose "home".

11. Then, under posts page, choose blog.

12. Enter how many blog pages you want to show on your website.

13. Click on "full text" to display the full text of each post.

14. Now, click on "save changes".

Separating your blog from the other sections makes it easier for your visitors to navigate your site. This allows them to easily locate your blog from your home page. It also gives your website a much more polished look.

Chapter 18: Static HomePage or Blog Posts? How To Change The Setting

A WordPress website can have a static or dynamic home page and blog posts. By default, WordPress displays your latest posts on your home page. This is called the "dynamic home page". Some website owners prefer what we call a "static home page". This is a custom home page that does not feature your latest posts. This is particularly useful for people who wants to separate their blog from their website. But, why would you want to separate your blog posts from your website?

Well, for one, separating your blog posts from the other pages in your site makes your website look more professional. The static home page is usually used by businesses as it allows them to showcase their products instead of their blog posts.

First, you need to create a home page following the process outlined in chapter 15. Then, click on "reading" at the left side of the screen.

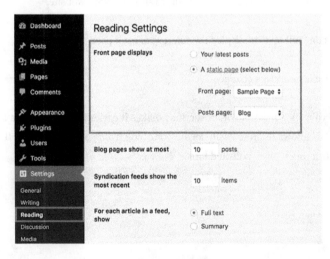

Photo Source: wpbeginner.com

Click on the "static page" radio button. Then, enter "home page" next to "front page". Save changes and you're done.

Remember that any WP page can be used as a "static front page". But, you need to publish a page first before you can use it as a static front page.

Chapter 19: How To Allow and Disallow Comments

Placing a comment section on your posts allow your readers and customers to give you feedback. But, spammers also use these section to post malicious links. If you're trying to grow your business and connect with your customers, it's best to allow comments on your posts, by following these steps.

1. Log in to your WordPress account.

2. Go to settings.

3. Then, click on the discussion tab.

4. Go to default settings and make sure that the "allow people to post comments on new articles" box is ticked. Don't tick it if you want to disallow comments on your posts.

Photo Source: en.support.wordpress.com

Then, click on "save settings".

If you're running a blog, it may be a good idea to allow comments so you can engage with your audience and encourage them to give a feedback. But, if you're running a business website, it's probably best to disable the comments section on your pages. This makes your website look more business-like and professional.

Chapter 20: How To Add Media and Edit Images in Your Media Folders Using WordPress Images Editor

Photos and videos add visual value to your website. But, before you add photos and videos to your website, you must follow these rules:

1. Add photos and videos that are related to the content of your site.
2. Add photos that are compatible with your site design.
3. Make sure to use uncopyrighted images and videos. Always include your source.
4. Try to use original photos as much as you can.
5. Make sure that the image that you use are clear.

Add Images

To add media to your post, click on "add media" which is located at the top left corner of your post toolbar.

Photo Source: en.support.wordpress.com

Click on "add new". You can also click on "add via URL" if your image is displayed on another website.

Upload the photos that you want to include in your website. Then, click on the photos that you want to insert to your post. Click on "continue".

Photo Source: en.support.wordpress.com

Go to the "layout" and then choose the photos layout you want. If you're going to use multiple photos, it's best to make a collage. To do so, click on multiple photos, go to "layout" then click on either "tiled mosaic" or "square tiles".

Photo Source: en.support.wordpress.com

Click on the "insert" button to insert the photos to your post.

Edit Images

Yes, there are a lot of amazing photo editing software. But, you can edit your images in WordPress, too, by following these steps:

1. Go to "add media".

2. Click on "add new" and then, upload the photo you want to edit.

3. Click on the photo that you want to edit and a pop up will appear. Click on the "edit image" button located at the lower left side of the pop up.

4. You'll see a menu with basic photo editing options like rotate, flip, and crop.

5. Use these buttons to edit your images.

6. Once you're done, click on save.

It's that easy!

Add Video

If you are a life coach or a fitness coach, adding a video on your website will help you introduce yourself to your potential clients.

To add a video to your post, upload your video in your YouTube channel. You can embed most videos in YouTube, just make sure to give credit where credit is due.

Go to the bottom part of the video and click on "share". Now, you'll see the link of the video. Copy that link and then, go to the Wordpress admin panel of your website.

Go to "posts" located at the left side of your screen. Then, click on "add new". Enter the title of the post. **Go to the text editor tab and click "paste". Now click on the icon below so the video does not appear as a "clickable link".**

Photo Source: agentWP.com

Then, click on save and publish. You're done!

Add Audio

To add an audio file to your self-hosted WordPress website, you need to install and activate a plugin called "oEmbed HTML5 audio".

After you activate the plugin, go to "posts" and click on "add new". Now, click on "add media" to upload the audio file from your computer. You can only upload wav, mp3, and ogg formats. Once you have uploaded the file, copy the file location.

Photo Source: wpbeginner.com

Then, paste the URL on your post. The plugin will automatically use an HTML5 audio tag to embed the file to your post. Click on "save" and "publish".

People these days have short attention spans and they do not have the time to read your blog posts. This is the reason why adding media to your posts will help hook your readers and increase your site traffic.

Chapter 21: Adding Meta Tags to Posts

Meta tags are the description that you'll see below your URL at the search engine results page of Yahoo, Google, or any other search engine.

Meta can act as a "click bait". So, it is important to write a meta tag that aptly describes your business or organization. If you strategically place "keywords" on your meta tags, it can help improve your website visibility, too, and increases your website rank on the search engine results page. This means that when a person types your targeted keyword on Google, they'll instantly see your website.

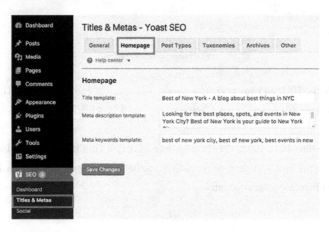

Photo Source: wpbeginner.com

To edit the meta tag of your posts or pages, make sure that you installed Yoast SEO. Then, go to the Yoast SEO section at the bottom of your post. You can also click on the Yoast SEO button located at the left side of your screen.

Photo Source: wpbeginner.com

Click on "edit snippet" and then enter your targeted keywords under "meta keywords".

Now, add your SEO title – this is your title tag. Make sure to place your keywords on both your meta tag and title tag.

Type in your meta tag under meta description. Make sure that your description is catchy and well-written. Also, take note that the optimal length of a meta tag is between 130 to 160 characters (including spaces). Search engines usually crop out posts with meta descriptions that are longer than the optimal length.

SEO title

Editor's Pick of The Best Coffee Shops in New York City

Slug

best-coffee-shops-in-new-york-city

Meta description

Are you looking for the best coffee shops in New York City? We have hand-picked some of the best coffee shops in New York City for you to visit.

Close snippet editor

Now, click on save changes.

Chapter 22: Customizing Your Sidebar in the Widgets Section

Widgets are small programs that you can install on your blog or website. They can benefit your websites in many ways. You can use them to track web visitors, provide an interactive experience to your site visitors, and display ads on your site.

But, how do you use widgets and customize your widget sidebars? Well, to use the widgets feature, you'll have to follow these steps:

1. Go to "appearance".

2. Go to "widgets".

3. Choose a widget and drag it to your sidebar. You can place it wherever you wish.

4. Once you're done, WP automatically updates your theme.

5. Now, preview your site and make sure that the widget is in the right place.

6. Go back to the "widges" section to add more widgets.

7. You can simply arrange the widgets by dragging them around.

8. You can customize the widget by clicking on the arrow next to it to expand its interface.

9. Click on "save".

10. If you want to remove it, you can simply click on "delete" or "remove".

To customize your sidebars:

1. Go to "theme settings".

2. Then, go to "general settings" and then, click on "custom sidebars".

3. Write down the alias for your sidebar, e.g. contact us, FAQ, etc.

4. Click add more aliases if you wish to add new alias names.

5. When you're done, click on "save".

6. Go to "appearance" and then click on "widgets".

7. You will now see the list of custom sidebars.

8. You can just drag and drop the widgets into your custom side bar.

9. Now, assign the custom side bar to a post by clicking on "add new page", go to "page layout", and then, "choose sidebar".

10. Choose the custom side bar from the select options.

Now, you're done!

Chapter 23: How to Check Your Site's Raw Analytics from cPanel in your Hosting Account

Your WordPress self-hosted website comes with raw analytics that contain important data about your website like site traffic. You can access this data by following these steps:

1. Login to cPanel.

2. Now, go to the "metrics" section.

3. Click on "raw access".

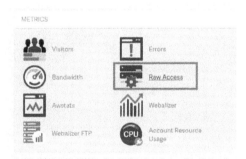

4. You will see "download current access logs". You'll see the list of the domain names in your hosting account. Select the domain you want to view statistics for.

5. Your browser will begin downloading your compressed access log.

6. Once the download is complete, uncompress the file and open it.

There's another way to view your website traffic and that's through Google Analytics which we will discuss in the next chapter.

Chapter 24: How To Add Tracking Codes to Your WordPress Site Using A Free Plugin

Google Analytics is a free reporting service that you can use for the marketing campaign of your business. It provides extensive data that includes your website traffic and the profile and location of your site visitors. This information is useful if you plan to run a Google or Facebook ad.

Google Analytics allows you to identify what people are searching for in your site. It also helps to detect your best and worst performing posts. So, you'll know what kind of content your customer wants.

But, to install Google Analytics, you need to add a tracking code to your site with a plug in. To do this, you'll need access to your site's FTP. You'll also need a live WordPress installation running on your theme and a code/text editor like Filezilla.

1. Check your theme's "header.php" file to make sure that you have the "wp_head" hook.

   Your plugins will insert a code to your website by attaching a code to a hook called "wp_head". This hook is used to insert styles, scripts, and more.

   To check if you have a "wp_head", go to your FTP. Open your wp-content file. Now, choose the folder that contains your themes, the folder usually starts with wp-content/themes/. Now, open a file called header.php. You will find the wp_head hook at the bottom of the <head> section of your file.

   If your head.php file does not contain the hook, add the code w_head before </head>.

2. Get your Google analytics code.

Go to https://analytics.google.com and click on sign up. This will take you to the new account page. Fill out that form.

Then click on "get tracking ID".

You'll get your tracking code. Copy everything from <script> and </script>

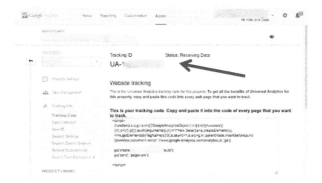

3. Create the plugin.

Now it's time to create the plugin where you add the tracking code to. Go to your wp-content/plugins folder. Click on "create a new PHP file" and name it something like wpmudev-analytics.php.

Open that file using your code editor. Now, add this code:

```php
<?php
/*
Plugin Name: Simple Google Analytics Plugin
Plugin URI: http://yourdomainname.com
Description: Adds a Google analytics tracking code to the <head> of your theme
Author: Your Name
Version: 1.0
*/
?>
```

Then, this code:

```php
<?php
function wpmudev_analytics ( ) { ?>

<?php }
add_action( 'wp_head', 'wpmudev_analytics', 10 );
```

This attaches your analytics to the hook. Now, it's time to activate your plugin.

4. Activate your plug in.

Now, let's say that this is your Google analytics tracking code:

```
<script type = "text/javascript">

    var _gaq = _gaq II [];

    _gaq.push(_setaccount', PA-XXX');

    _gaq.push (_trackpageview);


    (function() {

    var = document.createelement ('script'); ga type = "text/javascript"; ga.sync
=true

    ga.src = ('https:' = document.location.protocol? 'https://ssl':

</script>
```

Copy the tracking code to function script so it looks like this:

```
<?php
function wpmudev_analytics ( ) { ?>


    <script type = "text/javascript">

        var _gaq = _gaq II [];

        _gaq.push(_setaccount', PA-XXX');

        _gaq.push (_trackpageview);
```

```
(function() {

    var = document.createelement ('script'); ga type = "text/javascript";
ga.sync =true

    ga.src = ('https:' = document.location.protocol? 'https://ssl':

</script>
```

```
<?php }

add_action( 'wp_head', 'wpmudev_analytics', 10 )
```

Now, save your plug-in file. Go to your site admin page and go to "plugins". You should see your new plugin. Click on "network activate" to activate your plugin.

Wait for a few hours or a few days before Google picks up your tracking code.

Chapter 25: Set Up Traffic Analytics Using JetPack

You can also set up traffic analytics by using JetPack. When you log in to your WordPress dashboard, you'll see Jetpack at the center portion of your screen. But what is it? Well, it's a collection of plugins. It has a number of functionalities. It allows you to access reports, build a contact form, add a comment section to your posts, and allow visitors to subscribe to your blog.

First, you need to login to your WordPress account. Then, go to plugins. Search for "Jetpack 4.6". As of writing, this is the latest version of the plugin. This plugin is compatible with PHP 7.1 and it allows Google Analytics integration.

Click on "install now" and then, click on "activate plugin". The good news is that WordPress stats is automatically enabled when you activate Jetpack. To manually activate it, just go to your dashboard. Then, go to "screen options" and then, check the box beside site stats.

Photo Source: jetpack.com

You'll then see your site traffic stats on your dashboard.

Photo Source: jetpack.com

If you want to check your top performing posts and pages, go to "view old stats". If you want to see more details about your visitors, click on "view more stats on WordPress.com)". This allows you to check the location of your visitors.

The good news is that you can use your WordPress.com stats with Google Analytics. If you have installed Jetpack, you can simply go to your dashboard. Then, go to "Jetpack". Go to "settings", then "traffic". Then, go to "Google analytics". Now, go to https://analytics.google.com/analytics/web/provision/?authuser=0#provision/SignUp / to sign up for a new account. Fill out the form. Then, copy the tracking code.

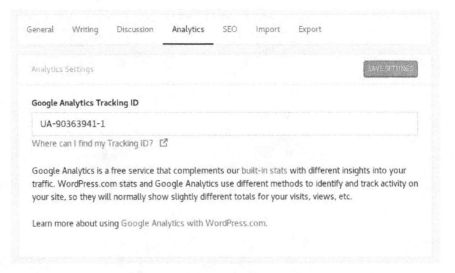

Then, click on save settings. Wait for a few hours or a few days to view your analytics data.

Chapter 26: How to Set Up Your Domain Email Account in cPanel

Using your own domain name email adds credibility to your business. It strengthens your brand and it helps build customer trust. This also gives you maximum momentum.

You can create your own domain email account by following these steps:

1. Go to your "cPanel".

2. Then, click on "email accounts" located in the email section.

3. Enter the details of your new email account. Then, click on "create account".

4. Then, you'll get a notification that the account has already been created.

5. Now, go back to your cPanel dashboard. Go to the mail section. Click on "forwarders".

6. Fill out the form.

Photo Source: problogger.com

7. Click "add forwarder".

8. Now, integrate your new domain email with your Gmail.

9. Sign in to Gmail.

10. Go to options.

11. Click on mail settings.

12. Click on "accounts and imports".

13. Check "send mail as".

14. Then, click on "add another email address you own".

15. A pop up will appear. Enter the domain name that you just created.

16. Click on "next".

17. Click on "send verification".

18. Check your email inbox to see the verification email.

19. You can send a sample email to see that the changes were complete.

Conclusion

I hope that this book was able to help set up your self-hosted WordPress website or at the very least give you a better understanding of how to set up your own wordpress hosted domain with full 100% control. Having a WP site is truly useful for bloggers and small business owners. Wordpress is a great web application to help launch your business or blogging career without having to learn website coding or technology upfront.

But, remember these tips:

✓ Purchase a domain name that represents your brand or business.

✓ If you have the extra budget, you may want to also purchase the extensions associated to your .com domain such as the .net, .co, .biz, and .org. This will help protect your brand from scrupulous people who want to ride on your brand's popularity and credibility.

✓ Do not give your "account management panel" username and password to your web developer as this contains your billing and credit card information.

✓ If you are aiming to build a high traffic website, it's best to go for VPS(virtual private server) hosting. But, if you're on a budget then you may want to go for shared hosting. Remember, Wordpress does use a good amount of memory because of it operates on a database structure, your pages are dynamic not static, theres more work going on versus a plain static html website.

✓ Use plugins to increase your website functionality but don't overload your site with too many plugins unless you have LOTS of memory and space. Plugins should be kept at bare minimums.

✓ Invest in SSL certificate if you're running an online shop. This helps protect your customer information. This also increases your site's credibility and protection. Most good web hosting companies are offering a free SSL with a new account. Only use 3rd party verified SSL certificates, they are the most trusted. Self-signed certificates do not fully authenticate.

Finally, if you enjoyed this book, then I'd like to ask you for a favor, would you be kind enough to leave a review for this book on Amazon? It'd be greatly appreciated!

And we're not done yet! Scroll down to access the bonus section of this book!

Thank you and good luck!

Bonus Section: Secret Tips I Wish Someone Told Me When I Started WordPress

Yes, we are not done yet! There's more. When I started my first WordPress website, there's a lot of things that I didn't know. Here's a list of the things that I wish I knew before I used WordPress. I outlined them for you, so you won't commit the same mistakes that I did when I launched my first self-hosted WP website.

Buy A Verified SSL Certificate

If you're running an online store, you want to make sure that you build a safe and secure website environment for your customers. So, it's a good idea to get web security. The internet is generally good as it gives you access to truckloads of information. It also allows you to connect with people all over the world. But, the internet is filled with bad people, too.

In fact, there are a number of people who would try to steal your customer's important information like credit card numbers, pins, and social security numbers. If customers don't feel safe in your site, they won't buy the products that you're selling. So, you need to secure your website using an SSL certification.

Have you noticed that some websites begin with "https". This means that the website has what we call SSL security.

SSL is the acronym for Secure Socket Layer. It is a technology that secures sensitive data like passwords and credit cards by encrypting this information while it passes through the server. So, it can't be intercepted.

If you have an SSL certificate, you are telling your visitors that your website is secure. An SSL certificate is also a proof that you are the legitimate owner of your website. So, in a way, it increases your website's and business' credibility.

You can purchase your SSL certificate from the following providers (we recommend COMODO)

- ✓ Digicert – Digicert is used by the top websites such as Facebook, Amazon, NASA, Yahoo, and Wikipedia.
- ✓ VeriSign – If you want maximum security, you should go for VeriSign as they can do up to 256 bit encryption. But, they are a bit expensive.
- ✓ GeoTrust – Offers basic encryption for $299.
- ✓ **Comodo** – Offers SSL certificates for just about anybody – from blogs to e-commerce websites.
- ✓ GoDaddy –GoDadddy is the biggest domain registration site. They also offer SSL certificates.

Best Tip: Get the "Duplicate Page" Plugin To Quicly Churn Out Templated Web Pages In WordPress.

You want consistency in your web design so sometimes, you use template webpages to achieve this.

Duplicate Page is a plugin that you can use to duplicate your pages and posts in just one click. You just need to install this plugin. Then, activate it. Go to "Duplicate Page Settings" from the settings tab. Then go to "Create New Post/Page". Then, after typing your content, you'll see the "duplicate this post/draft" option.

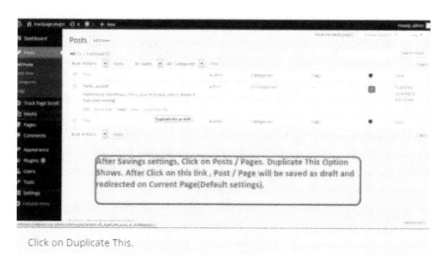

Click on Duplicate This.

Click on that and voila! You'll see the duplicate of your post.

Security Tips

Your website serves as the online "front desk" of your business. So, it has to be secured. Here's a list of top security tips that can protect your website from attackers:

1. Use strong passwords.

We all know that we are supposed to use strong passwords. But, we end up using a password that's easy to remember and easy to hack. To protect your website from hackers, you have to follow these tips:

- ✓ Use a unique password for **each account**.
- ✓ Do not use your name, birthday, or other personal information as your password.
- ✓ Make sure that your backup password information and options are updated.

2. Use HTTPS.

Getting an SSL certificate is one of the best things that you can do for your website.

3. Install a security plugin.

Install a security plugin to keep your site safe from malware and brute-force attacks. Here's a list of the best WordPress security plugins that you can use:

- ✓ Sucuri Security – This offers continuous malware scanning. It stops DDoS attacks and hacks immediately. It also provides help for hacked websites.

- ✓ Jetpack – This plugin protects your website from brute-force attacks from hackers and botnets. It also notifies your site whenever you have a downtime.

✓ WPS Hide Login – This is a simple plugin that prevents brute force attack.

✓ **All In One WP Security & Firewall** – This plugin has a password strength tool that helps you and your site visitors create strong passwords. It also has a one-click database backup. It also includes a firewall that protects against XSS or Cross Site Scripting.

✓ Shield Security – This plugin blocks suspicious URLs. It also provides security against brute force attacks.

✓ Updraft Plus – This enables you to backup your website and upload it to cloud service providers like Google Drive and Dropbox.

4. Tighten the network security of your website.

If your website is maintained by various people in your office, you need to tighten your network security. You have to ensure that passwords are changed frequently and that logins expire after a short period of time.

5. Hide your admin page.

Use robot_txt file to discourage Google from listing your site admin page.

Your website represents your brand and your company. So, you must make security a priority.

How to Remove or Change The Theme Author Name At Footer Using The HTML Editor Option

There are two ways to change the theme author name at the footer. You can change it through CSS or you can do it through an HTML text editor. But, you should avoid the CSS method at all cost as it's going to mess up your site SEO.

To change the theme author name through your HTML text editor, you should follow these steps:

1. Log in to your WordPress dashboard and then click on the "editor"

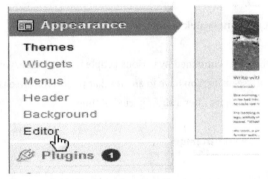

Photo Source: inmotionhosting.com

2. Now, click on "Footer" to edit your footer.php link.

3. Find the code that shows the text at the bottom. Which looks like the highlighted text:

```
<div class="site-info">
        <?php
            /**
             * Fires before the footer text for footer customization.
             *
             */
            do_action
        ?>
        <span class="site-title"><a href="<?php echo esc_url(
home_url( '/' ) ); ?>" rel="home"><?php bloginfo( 'name' );
?></a></span>
            <a href="<?php echo esc_url( __( 'https://wordpress.org/',
'twentysixteen' ) ); ?>"><?php printf( __( 'Proudly powered by %s',
'twentysixteen' ), 'WordPress' ); ?></a>
        </div><!-- .site-info -->
```

You can either change it to your company name or you can remove it.

4. Click on update.

Add The Auto Legal Pages Plug In

Legal pages increases your website credibility. Search engines like Google also prefer to index websites with legal pages. So, it is best to add auto legal pages plug in such as the "WP Legal Pages". This plugin includes privacy policy, DCMA policy, and EU cookie policy. The premium version of this plug in includes:

- ✓ Linking policy
- ✓ Facebook privacy policy
- ✓ Cookie policy template
- ✓ Anti-spam policy
- ✓ Terms and conditions
- ✓ Affiliate agreement
- ✓ Refund policy

The pages that you create using this plug in are easy to edit and modify. The plug in also has a force agreement option. This means that you can force your users to agree to the terms.

This plug in is easy to use and the free option is already packed. So, you won't have to upgrade to the premium version.

How to Retrieve Your WordPress Web Login PassWord From Your Back-End Hosting Account in PHP MyAdmin – A Life Saver

If you don't update your website frequently, you'll most likely forget your password. But, the good news is, you can retrieve or reset your password using PHP MyAdmin by following these steps:

1. Log in to your server admin account. It can be through Hsphere, Plesk, or cPanel.
2. Open your PHP MyAdmin.
3. Then, go to your WebPress database.
4. Click on wp_users at the left side of the screen.

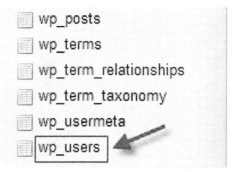

Photo Source: wexplorer.com

5. You will see all your usernames and passwords.

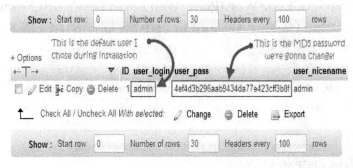

Photo Source: wpexplorer.com

6. Check the user "admin" to retrieve your WP admin password.

How to Back Up Your WordPress Site Using The Visual Installer Softaculous – This Stays On Your Hosting Account

Softaculous is a script library that automates the installation of open source and commercial applications to your website. Scripts found in softaculous are executed from the admin area of the site control panel via an interface tool like Plesk, H-Sphere, DirectAdmin, InterWorx, and ISP manager.

You can use it to install over 50 apps on your website. You can also use it to back up your website.

To do this:

1. *Go to your cPanel account.*
2. *Check the software and services section and click on "Softculous".*
3. *On the top area of your screen, click on "application installs".*
4. *Go through the list of applications and then click on the backup icon.*
5. *Click on Backup Database.*
6. *Then, click the "backup installation" button located at the bottom part of the screen.*
7. *A progress bar will appear on your screen. Then what's it's completed, you'll see a message saying that your backup was created successfully.*

To download the backup that you just created, you just have to follow these steps:

1. Go to your "cPanel".
2. Go into the software and services section and then, click on "softculous".
3. Click on the "backup and restore" link at the upper right portion of your screen.
4. Now, click on the file name of the backup that you created.

5. Once, you downloaded the backups you need, remove the backups that you no longer need. Clicking the "x" icon next to the file you want to remove.

How to Make A Multi-Site Network and Why This Can Be Super Useful For WorkGroups With Multiple Bloggers

Networking is important in any kind of business, even in blogging. WordPress allows you to create a network of websites using its "multisite" feature.

Creating a multi-site network is like creating your own "WordPress.com". This allows you to run as many sites as you want.

The multisite feature has a lot of benefits and applications. This feature comes in handy to companies who manages various brands. Let's say that you're a wellness company that sells honey, essential oil perfumes, sunblocks, and yoga mats. The WP multisite feature allows you to efficiently manage the website of each of your product line. You can also use it to create a network of bloggers.

Here's what you need to do to create a network within your WordPress site:

1. Prepare your WP site before you enable the multisite feature. This is because your website will be updated once you create a network. So, it is wise to backup your files. You also need to deactivate your active plugins. You can reactivate them after you create the multisite network.
2. Enable the multisite feature in your wp-config.php file. Open the file and add this code above the first line:

/*Multisite*/
Define ('WP_ALLOW_MULTISITE', true);

You also have to adjust your memory settings in the PHP.INI file in your web host root directory to maximize your website load speed.

You'll often encounter the "exhausted memory error" when you're using WordPress or any other free open source PHP program. When you encounter this error, you need to change the memory limit in your php.ini file by following these steps:

1. Go to your "cPanel".
2. Go to the file section and look for the file manager.

Photo Source: inmotionhosting.com

3. Select the PHP.INI file and then use the code editor to edit the file. Add this script:

```
memory_limit = 64M
```

Remember that the maximum memory that a script may consume is 64 MB, so make sure to set your memory limit to 64 MB.

4. Once you're done, click on "save changes.

How to Set Your WordPress Site To Auto-Update The Themes, Plugins, and Even When A New Version of WordPress Comes out

Keeping your website updated at all times increases the stability and security of your site. It also helps to take advantage of the cool features that comes with the latest version of WordPress. It also increases your website speed and fixes bugs.

To auto-update all your plugins whenever a new version of WordPress comes out, simply add this code to your site's specific plug in or php file:

add_filter('auto_update_plugin', '_return_true')

If you also want to auto-update your theme once a new version comes out, simply add this code:

add_filter('auto_update_theme', '_return_true')

WP also give you the option to do this in the softaculous dashboard within your cPanel account.

Resources

Fastest & Cheapest Wordpress Hosting Plans
https://Internetweb.host

Elegant Themes – Wordpress Theme Club Full License & Security Updates
Click Here To See

Domains For Sale
https://NexGenDomains.com